SOMETIMES IT'S OK TO TELL SECRETS

A Book for Parents and Children to Read Together

Written by
Amy C. Bahr

Illustrated by
Frederick
Bennett Green

GROSSET & DUNLAP

Copyright © 1986 by RGA Publishing Group, Inc. and Frederick Bennett Green. Concept by
RGA Publishing Group, Inc. IT'S OK TO SAY NO is a trademark of RGA Publishing Group, Inc.
Published by Grosset & Dunlap, a member of The Putnam Publishing Group, New York.
Printed in Italy. Published simultaneously in Canada. Library of Congress Catalog
Card Number: 85-080576 ISBN 0-448-15325-4 A B C D E F G H I J

NOTE TO PARENTS

As responsible parents, we protect our children by teaching them the rules and regulations of water safety, fire safety, and bicycle safety. The IT'S OK TO SAY NO Picture Books will help you teach your child the most important safety lesson of all—body safety.

As you read this book with your child, or with a child you care about, you may want to expand on some of the situations, or you may prefer to read the simple text just as it is. In either case, this book should stimulate discussion. It's important that you take the time to let your child respond to questions asked in the book, and that you listen to any questions the child may have. If you feel awkward or embarrassed, you should direct these questions to someone you and your child feel comfortable with. Above all, the child must understand and remember the rules that will help him or her to recognize and respond to threatening situations.

The IT'S OK TO SAY NO Picture Books are not meant to scare but rather to educate. Children need to learn the words and phrases in the books and use them to say no, to tell their parents if something is wrong, and to avoid dangerous situations. Adults, in turn, must learn to listen and must give their children the freedom to tell.

—The Children's Justice Foundation, Inc.

Did you ever keep a secret?

Some secrets are fun to keep. Your mom's birthday present is that kind of secret.

It's fun to keep it a secret if you have an imaginary friend.

If something special happens to you, you might keep it a secret.
When you finally tell, everyone is happy and proud and surprised.

If you do something wrong, you might keep it a secret for a while. But telling that kind of secret is better than lying or worrying or feeling bad.

You might keep a secret because you're ashamed. But a secret that makes you feel unhappy is not OK.

That is the kind of secret you should tell right away. Sometimes a grownup can help, even if *you* think *nobody* can.

You might keep a secret because someone tells you to. What if your babysitter gives you a present and asks you not to tell your parents?

Tell your mom or dad about the present anyway. No one should ask you to keep a secret from your parents.

What if a teenager asks you to join his secret club? What if you're supposed to do everything he says because he's the president?

Tell your mom or dad about the club, even if you promised you wouldn't tell.

What if you see a grownup acting weird or hanging around where he shouldn't be? You should always tell about something that looks strange to you.

You should always tell about something that you know is wrong.
Tell your mom or dad or another grownup.

What if your teacher does something that makes you feel weird or yucky? What if he says, "This is our little secret. I won't like you anymore if you tell"?

When an adult is doing something wrong, he will ask you not to tell. But you don't have to keep a secret just because an adult asks you to.

Tell your parents about your teacher anyway, even if you think they're going to be mad.

What if an older kid pulls down your pants and makes you cry?
What if he says he'll hurt you if you tell anyone?

Tell anyway. Never keep a scary secret all by yourself.

What if someone touches your private parts and says you have to keep it a secret? What if he says you'll get in trouble if you tell anyone? What if he says your parents won't believe you if you tell them?

No matter what he says, you should tell a grownup you trust.
Even if it's hard to talk about, keep telling until you find someone
who will listen and understand. Maybe you can tell the person
who reads this book with you.

If you have a problem, keeping it secret can make it seem much worse than it is.

Sometimes a grownup can help if you tell what's worrying you.

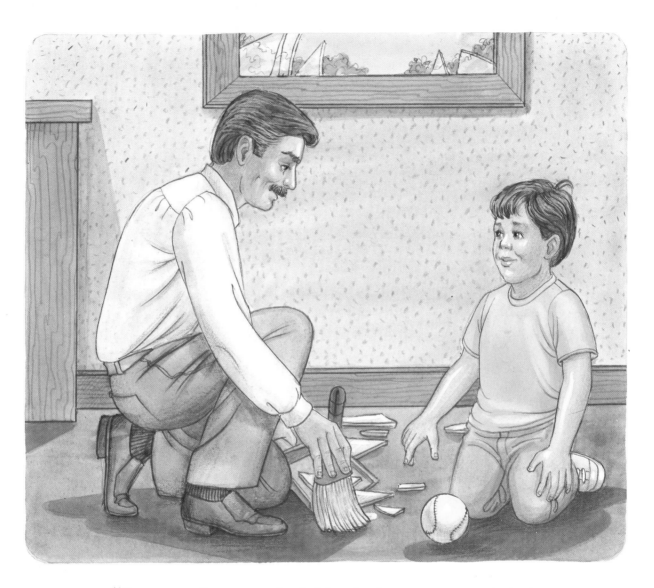

When you tell a secret that's been bothering you, you feel a lot better.

Don't keep secrets with grownups, unless the secret is really a happy surprise.

Remember, secrets are for fun, not for making you worry.

Now you know that sometimes it's OK to tell secrets!